Managing your Home
A comprehensive guide to caring for your home and family

Written and compiled by Nichola Williams

Published by Good Grounds Media LTD®

ISBN 978-0-9928873-2-2

Cover design: Nichola Williams

Managing your Home
A comprehensive guide to caring for your home and family

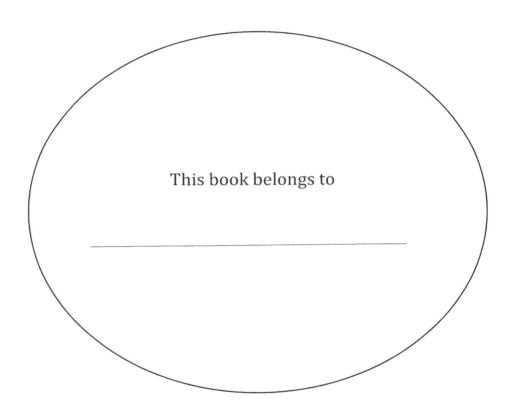

This book belongs to

_____

Acknowledgements

I dedicate this book to every wife and mother who has been given the task of managing their home. I would like to especially mention the following women who inspire me every day by the way they love their homes and families. Ladies you have always made me feel incredibly proud to be a homemaker. Unknowingly, you have lifted me up on days when I have felt overwhelmed.

Adlyn Barrett
Claire Cameron-Lewis
Laura Kartal
Natalie Green
Neala Okuromade
Sheila Nzisa
Stacey Gewitzke

Contributors

I would also like to thank the following ladies for sharing their wisdom with me and allowing me to include it in this book. Ladies you have no idea how much I love you.

Marcia Aka-Kadjo

Danielle Edie

Sandra Edie

Annie Odogwu

Aida Ghebretensae

Natasha Corbett

Contents

Introduction

~

As the saying goes, there's no place like home. I believe that in no other setting is there a dynamic like that of in a home. It can be a place that is filled with love, laughter and life. Where individuals are able to thrive and flourish. It can also be a place filled with contention, frustration and strife where chaos is the norm and productivity is non-existent. The quality of the environment in your home is subject to many factors but you will find that it largely depends on how you manage it. For the last twelve years my primary responsibility has involved being a stay at home wife and mother to five children. This comes with a tremendous work load that can be both physically and mentally draining. It can also be one of my biggest sources of joy.

If you own or rent a home, then its upkeep is *your* responsibility! If you are married or have a partner then the responsibility is most definitely shared and if you have children, I advise that they take part in executing what it takes to keep a positive home environment. If the day to day running and maintenance of systems is largely down to you, I'm hoping that you'll find this book helpful.

It is fair to say that home life is not always easy. There will most certainly be times of disagreement, hardship and disappointment, but these need not be the experience for the majority of the time. Imagine your home like a haven, a place to retreat to even during the tough seasons. I believe that a quality, healthy, thriving environment is largely dependent on two factors:

1. The physical upkeep of the home
2. Maintaining quality relationships

You would be surprised how much the physical upkeep of the home matters. Whether you are a very tidy person with clear-cut preferences or a lot more laid back when it comes to cleanliness and order, maintaining the home is key. Ultimately the way you run your home is up to you but my hope is that the tips and advice written in these pages will aid you in that process. In this book you will find some practical tips and information about how to manage your home effectively that has been collected from women from a variety of backgrounds and in different seasons of life. None of us are perfect at keeping house so regardless of how organised things appear to be when reading through the chapters, not everything will work all of the time. Much of its contents are things I have tried, tested and do regularly but not all the time. Sometimes life has a lot going on but however busy you find yourself, it is worth taking time and effort to invest in the place you call home.

Nichola -x-

Begin here: What type of Home?

~

A helpful place to start when wanting to manage the home well, involves some thinking space. It may be wise to set aside time to think about the kind of home that you would like. Before implementing anything, you should do this with a husband or partner if you have one and you may also want to hold a family meeting to get children on board. To kick this activity off, make a list of adjectives that reflect the home you envision.

Examples

Warm	Welcoming	Empowering
Spacey	Peaceful	Immaculate
Airy	Organised	Cosy
Neat	Inviting	Clean
Tidy	Successful	Friendly

Next, ask yourself some useful questions regarding the current operation and functionality of your home. The aim of this is to get you to do an assessment of the quality and running of your home at the moment. This will make it easier to pinpoint areas of strength and weakness.

Suggested questions to ask:

- Does my home serve the needs of my family?
- Is home a good place to work, play or live?
- Is it welcoming?
- Is it a place where people develop (instead of stagnating or being hindered)?
- Do family members receive peace, inspiration and support?
- Have I/we created a loving environment?
- What home improvement projects need completing in our home?
- What do I want people to leave my home feeling?
- How do I want to feel when I walk through the door?
- How would I like my children to remember home and family life once they have grown up?
- What would I like the next generation to adopt from the way I run my home?

Once you have completed answering the questions, write a short vision statement for your home. It need only be a sentence or two at the most:

"Our home is a home of love. A place where everyone is uniquely celebrated and free to express themselves respectfully."

"Our home is a home that nurtures people, potential and passion."

"Our family home will enable its members to realise their dreams and aspirations in order to positively impact the lives of others."

Display your vision statement somewhere that you can refer to it often. Consider putting it up publicly for other family members to see. The beauty of doing such an exercise is that it somewhat directs you in how best to run your home. For example, if you want a home in which family members always stay connected, then it may not be a good idea to put individual televisions in everyone's rooms as this could promote division.

The Importance of "Me" time

~

Managing your home is by no means an easy task. Running a home can be just as strategic as running a business, only we are emotionally invested in the people there, our family. Give your home the time, attention, effort and commitment it deserves. Successful homes and families do not happen by accident but are a result of focus, unity, deliberate and consistent actions. Decisions are constantly being made and hundreds of tasks carried out every week. When it comes to the daily running of a home there are a number of categories to consider:

1. **Investing in and maintaining relationships**
2. **Chores and cleaning**
3. **Managing routines and schedules**
4. **Administration and household accounts**
5. **Cooking and health management**
6. **Repairs and household developments**

Whether you are a homemaker who manages your home on a full time basis or juggle its upkeep and a job outside the home, it can be hard work. It is important that you prioritise time to rest and energise yourself regularly in order to stay on top of things. In the west, the pace of life is very fast and busyness is all too common. Gone are lazy Sundays when you would find only the local corner shop open for the morning, instead it has become an additional shopping day. Most major supermarkets and chain stores open on Sundays resulting in shopping activity being just as busy as other days. This has robbed much of the UK's people of what used to be somewhat of a 'national day of rest'. Additionally, with the development of the internet, mobile phones, social media and digital devices, we can be contacted instantly any time of the day or night. The benefit of this is that we are no longer subject to solely working from the office but instead can bring or set up the office wherever we are. On the down side, there is no running away from our commitments and as a result, family and private life can be infiltrated upon at the press of a button or swipe of a finger. Factoring in ample rest is becoming harder so we must be incredibly deliberate about it.

One of the things that will help us when it comes to managing our home effectively is setting ourselves up for success from the get go. Ensure that you are refuelling regularly to avoid running out of steam which will ultimately result in reduced productivity. What you do to refuel is totally up to you but I would recommend something little and often. Make sure you take one or two breaks during the day if you are at home full time, remember if you treat the running of your home like a job then you will give yourself a tea and lunch break. If you are working to task, then you deserve a break but don't be deceived that you will get things done if you have a habit of being lazy.

To ensure you get the most out of time for yourself you may want to consider or implement the following things:

- Everything doesn't have to be perfect – It's ok to allow a little clutter or mess
- Let yourself off the hook
- Learn to say no to anything that is unimportant to you or will negatively impact your home and family priorities
- Ask for help

- Get enough sleep
- Eat healthily
- Wake up, breathe and stretch - 5 mins
- Schedule non-appointment times
- Write a to-do list - This will get it all out of your head
- Write in a journal
- Enjoy reading
- Try taking the weekend off - I generally don't commit myself to anything on a Monday in order to recover from the busy weekend
- Delegate and outsource
- Acknowledge your limitations
- Reward yourself
- Be yourself

Suggestions for refuelling little and often:

1. Set yourself a luxurious bath with candles at the end of a hard working day
2. Take a 15 or 30-minute break with a hot drink and a magazine

3. Go for a 10-minute walk - the fresh air will do you some good
4. Go swimming or take a workout class once a week
5. Have working hours - Decide that you will work on the home until a specific time then stop. Check out completely and let the relaxation begin
6. Sit in silence and do nothing (my favourite thing to do)
7. Pamper yourself (or pay someone else to) e.g getting your nails painted or eyebrows shaped
8. Take a 5-minute break every hour

1

Investing in and maintaining relationships

*"Communication is essential in any relationship. I would always make time to talk to my kids and husband about anything or issues that may have an impact on the family. Spending family time together has also been important to me. I have always made it a point to have family outings or holidays when my children were younger. I would take an interest in any activities my children were involved in and set them additional maths and spelling tests." ~ **Sandra Edie***

Making time for your spouse

~

If you have a spouse, I believe that your marriage to him or her should be your highest priority human relationship, even above your children. This can sometimes be a hard pill for us to swallow but it has powerful truth attached to it. When I say above everyone else it simply means that your relationship is first. It is the primary relationship you give your energies to after your own well-being. I think it is worth taking a moment to remind ourselves of what most of us probably vowed on that wonderful day of our wedding:

*"[your name] do you take [spouse's name] to be your wedded husband/wife, to live together in marriage? Do you promise to love him/her, comfort him/her, honour and keep him/her for better or worse, for richer for poorer, in sickness and in health, and **forsaking all others**, be faithful only to him/her as long as you both shall live?"*

Now there are many adapted versions of these vows but the gist here is that you promised to put your husband first, as he did you. It is important that we remember this promise concerning the priority of our union. Maintaining the quality of your marriage is pivotal for keeping your

> *"For me and my husband Nicholas, we try to cook together, watch films, arrange date nights, speak about what we want and be honest if we are not happy with each other's actions or behaviour."*
>
> **~ Natasha Corbett**

family unit together, and strong. Statistics show that most families are stronger when there are two parents living under the same roof in a committed lifelong relationship. This however does not mean that you neglect your children's fundamental needs of love, care and support. We have a duty and a responsibility to parent our children lovingly, to parent them well. But often we can give our everything to the children, centre our whole existence around them and forget that before children there was a love relationship with someone. There are seasons in life when children can be particularly challenging or needy like the toddler years for instance so it can be difficult to place your marriage first. Sometimes it will seem near impossible! Chores, work, paying the bills and extended relatives can also get in the way if you let them.

How to keep your marriage a priority

Start and end the day together

Days are often busy. Some of us work a 35-50 hour job all week, we may be studying or have commitments outside of the home. Children have midweek activities, meals must be cooked and there are multiple errands to run. Between the vast array of activities, we can 'lose' each other whilst giving our energies to our many responsibilities. Starting the day together, even if only for a few minutes can do wonders. They can serve as reminders that despite the pressures of adult life, you are a team, doing life together. You can find out what is on the agenda for the both of you that day, pray for one another, share reminders and simply connect. Go to bed at the same time every night if you can. Cuddle, share a hot drink and enjoy the moment. Try your best to check-in at the start and end of every single day.

Have designated date nights

This is by no means easy to achieve but in my experience I can say that with some persistence this can be possible. For many years Harold and I struggled to have a date night. We have five children and at one point, all of them were under the age of ten-years-old! At that time it seemed as if our marriage was quickly getting lost amidst the many commitments that go with raising children. We decided that unless we did something quite drastic, we would be at risk of becoming total strangers. With that, date night was born. We earmarked Monday evenings as our time and regardless of how tired we were, it was going to happen. With some persistence and thankfully children who had quite a strict bedtime routine, within a few years it became a valuable unmissable event.

The key here was that we were deliberate. Even if you have very young children like we did and little support you can plan date nights indoors. Children will not be little and dependent forever so create a romantic environment in your living room or bedroom and share some quality time with your spouse. Setting aside a few hours every single week and sticking to it over time can be more effective than you think. Harold and I still have two children under twelve and we continue to spend date nights together. Our children expect to be kicked out of the living room on Monday evenings!

Find something you enjoy doing together

Sure it is okay to have the home and children in common but simply put, find something else. This could be a sport, movie watching, a creative hobby or something else. As long as it is something you both enjoy then eat your heart out. It is all too much of a tragedy that couples split once children have grown and flown the nest because they realised they shared little else. If you're stumped for what to do, maybe try a few different things and see which one you both enjoy the most. Harold and I have really liked cooking or baking together or even playing poker! At one point we would go and play tennis together. He decided to buy a set of quality rackets and teach me how to play. I didn't actually realise how much I enjoyed our games until after a few weeks when I started winning!

Go away, alone

This one may be the hardest to achieve if you have children or a small budget, both of which have been my experience at times. But with some careful planning ahead short breaks away could be a fantastic way to reconnect and focus on spending quality time together. You could opt for a long holiday, short city breaks or visit somewhere only a few hours away. As long as it allows you to focus solely on each other then it's a winner. I would recommend doing this annually where possible.

Laugh a lot

On a daily basis, it's okay to be silly. Life is boring if you are serious all of the time. Laugh. A lot. There is something special about the memories that are created when we laugh together and it makes you feel good and happy even during challenging times. Did you know that the critical laughing trigger is not a funny joke or movie? It is actually the company of another. The best laughter is social laughter. The involuntary kind that is communicated through two or more people that simply love each other's company. Reminisce on old times, muck around, play fight or play a game. However you do it, laugh.

Make time to listen to your spouse

Apparently women talk more than men. Sometimes that translates into a belief that men don't talk at all. It is a lie. Put a guy with a group of other guys who share an interest and there you will find some of the most vibrant conversations. Find out what interests your spouse and allow him or her space to share those interests with you. They may be in an area you neither care for or find interesting but they should be important to you because they are important to your spouse. Be interested in their work, skill, hobby or idea and find out more about the person you married!

> *"I would recommend **The 5 Love Languages** by Gary Chapman. This book has helped me so much and shown me how my husband and I have very different needs. My favourite resource has to be one by Mark Gungor and is called 'The Tale of Two Brains'. This video has helped me to understand my husband's brain & how he is wired as a man in greater detail. It's educational but with humour"*
> *~ Aida Ghebretensae*

Intentionally invest in your marriage

Take time to read books, watch and listen to resources and talk to other seasoned couples about what has made their marriage successful. Doing life with another human being who has had a different upbringing to you can be tricky at the best of times so don't panic when it doesn't mirror the Hollywood movies. This is real life!

Quality time with Children

~

There is nothing but benefits when it comes to the reasons I recommend quality time with children. Think of one of your dearest friends or relatives. Someone who you really connect with and love very much. If there is no one currently in your life like that, think back to when there was. I am willing to bet that a large part of why you are so close is because of the time you've spent with them, and not just being in close proximity but spending time being intimate. Intimacy is the glue that holds relationships together and our aim as parents should be to develop intimacy with our children. This affords them the opportunity to get to know us outside of being their provider and gives us a chance to understand them more deeply. I believe that being present with our children is very important for their identity.

Why you need to enjoy the season

We have all heard the saying "time flies" and often it really does seem to go quickly. Our children are born and we dream about the many things we will get to experience as they grow. A fifth birthday seems ages away but before you know it you are waving them off to school for their first day. Sometimes life gets tricky, the mundane or pressure of everyday living can obscure our view of what is really important. Tomorrow is never promised so embracing each day we are blessed with is where our focus should lie. Before children are born, we become desperate for them. Once they've arrived we enjoy having a baby but soon the toddler years come. All too often I hear parents say that they cannot wait until the children are in school (I have been guilty of this). The bottom line is that every age, stage and season, despite its challenges will have things we can and should celebrate. We celebrate them because when the season has gone, there is no way of getting it back. Allow children to jump in puddles and get muddy, they always seem to know just how to embrace every precious moment. They won't be small forever.

I try to communicate on a daily basis, I always ask my children to tell me how they feel today. I also have one-on-one time with them so we build a strong relationship not just as a family but also as a unique mother and child relationship. **- Danielle Edie**

If you have teenagers, apply the same school of thought. They won't be living with you forever so enjoy them. Often the teenage years are a time when we can clash the most with our children purely because they are becoming young adults. They want more freedom and control and we do not want to relinquish it. Pick which battles you are going to fight and overlook some of the others. A stomping of the feet or rolling of the eyes may not be a huge deal in the grand scheme of things. Choose what you can't ignore and let the rest slide. Remember that the closeness you share is what's really important.

Be deliberate

Ensure you set aside a specific day and time to spend with your child. This is most effective when done on some kind of regular basis e.g. once a week. What you choose to do with your child is up to you but make sure they have a say. There is nothing worse than making time to spend together and only one of you enjoys it. When I first implemented this I thought life was far too busy to spend quality time with each of my children every day. But then I broke it down and realised that if I spent ten minutes of quality time with each child individually, it only made a total of fifty minutes. Surely my life wasn't too busy to give my children fifty minutes of my day? I spent more time eating!

Once you decide on a day and time, follow through. I decided a long time ago that I needed to change something in my life if I was unable to spend just ten minutes a day with each of my children. Don't make empty promises and if the time must be changed, ensure you set another time during the same week, being careful not to cancel. It will then become something you both look forward to. My eight-year-old daughter often likes to spend time baking but my son who is fourteen would rather visit the cinema or go out shopping. The activities you choose may vary from child to child but it is important you do something he or she likes.

> *I try to make sure I spend quality time with my boys individually and also together. Benjamin and I will talk, do homework or play board games together. My toddler Nicholas and I will read together, and I'll pretend play with him. All three of us will maybe watch a film or sing and dance, or just have cuddles.*
>
> *~ **Natasha Corbett***

Family activities

As well as doing things separately, I'd have to say that shared activities are also great. My childhood was filled with family days out to the park, trips to restaurants, fun-filled holidays away from home, charades and board games at home. Family activities can help everyone stay connected, provide bonding and team building opportunities and create family stability. You could have a family day every week, monthly or bi-monthly. Every Sunday my family eat together around the television (instead of the dining table) and after chatting for a while we will pick a movie to watch (usually a funny one) and eat popcorn. Although this in itself is not what I would deem an activity to bring people together, the routine of it means that everyone expects to have a fun time with the family on a Sunday night. In addition, we go out several times a year to do something fun together. This year we are attending a large Christmas concert together!

Other suggestions:

Visit the cinema or theatre

Go bowling

Long walks

Visit a museum

Go for a river walk

Book a fun workshop

Go bike riding

Have a picnic

Extended Family Affairs

~

These days if you have extended family who you connect with, count yourself very blessed. The reality is that not everyone has this. Whoever you have in your life outside of your immediate household, even if it's one person, cherish them. Life gets busy, sometimes too busy and it is easy for us to forget about the importance of staying close to those we love. Even I am guilty of this. However, one thing that my parents did very well was teach my siblings and I how wonderful it is to have a family. We grew up knowing who most of our immediate family were and kept in close, regular contact with them. Even though we are now all adults, birthdays, christenings and family gatherings are the norm and our own children are used to it.

If you want to improve the relationships, you have with family please know that it does not happen overnight. You will have to cultivate your connection with them and over time bonding becomes easier. Make a point to schedule time together regularly in order to do this. One of the easiest ways to achieve this is by creating Family rituals. A family ritual is an activity that is repeated, deliberate, co-ordinated and has meaning. Anyone can create a family ritual but they are usually best started by someone in the family who genuinely has a heart to see the relationships flourish and improve. I would say that my mum is probably one such a person. She loves family and gets a lot of joy from seeing us all get together and get along. We have quite a few rituals but one of the main ones would be getting together at Christmas time. Traditionally, we gather together on Boxing day. Each household in the family will take it in turns to host everyone. Every year the family grows bigger yet we somehow manage to make it work regardless of the size of the property. I am convinced we will have to begin hiring a hall or hotel in the next few years. As new members have been added to us along the way some of us may have had to sacrifice attending (for example visiting a spouse's side of the family) but the rest of us gather together regardless. We know it happens, we expect it to happen and it would be very strange if we missed a year. It has become tradition. Other family rituals and traditions may revolve around birthdays, special occasions or some other common ground.

The point is to get together. Some things that you can do to help extended family remain closely knit include:

Inviting family members around for a meal.

This can be a planned affair or completely sporadic. There have been times that I've been on the phone to a sibling and they happen to be visiting my mum. I'll just decide to join the fun, add the children and before you know it, there is a full house. That is one of the benefits of living only a short walk or car journey away.

Send cards on birthdays, anniversaries, Christmas and other holidays.

Even if you don't live near one another, sending cards is a lovely way to remind family that you remember them and are there for them. Remembering special dates is a nice personal way to communicate that you care. Encourage children to join in by signing their name in your card or writing their own. If family send cards to you, phone up or send a text to say thank you.

Make phone calls

Call up simply to find out how someone is doing. Phone calls are so much more personal than a text message or email. This is particularly valuable to the older generation who didn't grow up with the beauty of the internet and all the wonders of digital technology. Video calling applications like skype are great for connecting with family that live quite a distance away or overseas because you can see one another, talk with multiple members and it costs next to nothing.

Share achievements and successes

Let one another know when wonderful things happen in your life. Graduation, a new job, house, passed a driving test or whatever it is. Sharing in this way allows others in and invites them to celebrate with you. Our family have a WhatsApp group where twenty-five of us regularly share small and big successes, photos, voice notes, social media posts and anything else worth talking or laughing about.

Really get to know them

Any great friendship requires time and attention. Though you may not be able to (or even want to) be friends with everyone, choose to develop intimacy with family. Be real with them and allow them the room to be real with you. All too often we can simply go through the motions and make small talk with family. Years go by and we don't really know one another. Blood may be thicker than water but it is possible to be closer with friends than family due to a failure to really connect. Spend quality time together going out, talking about and doing life with all its ups and downs. Be friends.

2
Chores and Cleaning

Finding time for cleaning

~

Regardless of whether you love cleaning or not, if you want a pest-free, germ-free, clear and sweet-smelling home, it must be done. Like anything else that we value we should be deliberate and make time to clean our homes. You may find that unless you deliberately do this, cleaning will not be a priority and it will be placed at the bottom of a long list of other things we have to do. Most of us learnt our cleaning skills throughout childhood and adolescence. Some may have been shown in detail how to keep house as part of regular family life. For others, perhaps mum, dad or some other adult did the majority of the chores and never passed on those essential skills to the children. Some may have grown up in a home with a maid or cleaner and others, a home where cleanliness was simply not a priority all together! Whatever your experience may have been, I would recommend doing some sort of cleaning daily, weekly, monthly and quarterly to keep your current home looking neat and respectable.

Educate yourself

There is a wealth of information available on the internet if you are completely clueless when it comes to cleaning. Women (and men) across the world have taken to documenting their cleaning routines and sharing their tips and tricks on a host of platforms. There are countless blogs to read, YouTube videos to watch and books you can purchase with step by step instructions to help you build up your skills. I would advise you fill yourself up with as much of this knowledge as you can. Although I competently manage my home, I am always on the lookout for ways to improve myself and. there is much I would like to do in my home that I have yet to accomplish. We must also remember that homes are forever changing. Children are born, grow up and leave. Husbands and wives change and grow older, we leave old jobs, get new jobs or go part-time, sickness may come or lives get busier. Being able to adapt cleaning routines to compliment these changes will be useful.

When you know what chores need to be done, it may be worth making a master list. Go into every room in your home and note down what tasks are needed to keep that room looking reasonably neat and tidy. By the time you've gone around the entire house, I would expect you'd have quite a lengthy master list. This task can be especially helpful when planning DIY projects or redecorating. I will explain more about this in section six of this book.

On the next page I have included some simple guidelines about how often cleaning should happen based on a vibrant, lived in home regardless of its size. A large family home with many members like mine will almost certainly require a lot more upkeep than a smaller apartment with only two or three living there. This information is only a guide and I would recommend you adapt it to suit your family and household needs.

What to do when

Daily chores: *Usually 1-2 quick whip rounds a day is needed. Perhaps one in the morning and another later on in the day. For example, these could take place after breakfast, after dinner and before bed. These times may be different if you work full time or are a full time homemaker. In addition, I would advise doing the following tasks. They should only take a few minutes each if done regularly.*

Place dirty laundry in hamper	Wiping kitchen counters (after use)	Cleaning the toilet, basin and bath/shower (after use)
Washing dishes (including loading/unloading dishwasher)	Wipe stove and microwave (after use)	Sweeping the floor
Making beds		Sort mail

Weekly chores: *The following chores may need to be done more than once a week depending on the size of your family or level of activity in your household. At the very least I would recommend these be completed once a week.*

Mopping hard floor surfaces	Hoovering carpets	Bathroom deep clean
Kitchen deep clean	Clean mirrors	Dusting surfaces and removing cobwebs
	Change bedlinen/sheets	
Clean fridge	Replenishing supplies (stationery, cosmetics, cleaning etc.)	Meal planning
Empty dustbins	Filing household paperwork	Change towels (more frequently if needed)
Laundry	Grocery shopping	
		Ironing

Monthly chores: *These are those house-cleaning tasks that shouldn't need to be done every week, but definitely need to happen regularly enough for a pleasant atmosphere.*

Deep clean bedrooms	Clean washing machine and/or dishwasher	Descale kettle
Wipe down walls	Wash cushion covers	Dust light fixtures
Hoover under furniture	Check smoke alarms	Clean oven
	Garden pruning	

Quarterly chores: *These tasks are usually needed to be done every three months or less. Some may only need doing twice a year.*

Clean windows	Wash net and heavy curtains	Deep clean fridge and freezer
Purge wardrobes of old clothing	Wash pillows/duvets	Turn and air mattresses

Enlist family members to help you with household chores, reminding them that you are a team and it is important that everyone pulls their weight. Go through your master list and decide what chores need other hands and feet to help or what can be done without your input. You may need to teach family members how to do chores through a coaching process or the creation of visual aids like checklists. This has worked especially well with my children who will quite easily forget the example. A checklist helps them remember the steps involved in completing a task. You may be in a position to rope in extended family members or neighbours to help you too. A friend of mine has a large family and needs some house help and neighbour to help her stay on track. There is absolutely nothing wrong with paying for help if you are able and if that is what is necessary to keep your home beautiful. Do not be made to feel guilty if you need it. Note that I stated 'house help' and not a nanny. If you enlist someone like a nanny or Au pair to help bring up your children remember that this person should not replace you as the parent. I personally believe that you should always remain the primary adult in your child's life.

Setting a Family Chores Rota

~

Unless you have no other commitments in life it is unlikely you will be able to maintain a home without some extra hands. Sometimes the easiest and most cost effective way of staying on top of the household chores and cleaning is to enlist the help of family members. A bit of hard graft never hurt children and there is something that everyone can pitch in on regardless of age. The best place to start is by taking a look at all the duties that need to be done and decide what needs hands and feet to help and what can be done without your input.

> *"My tip would be giving my children small manageable chores to do which help me. My 20 month old tidies up his toys and puts little things in the bins, like tissue or paper. My 7-year-old tidies his room, folds his clothes when he comes home from school. His two chores are emptying all the bins weekly and setting and tidying the table after mealtimes."* ~ **Natasha Corbett**

Decide which chores you are happy to delegate and how often they need to be done. Once you've done this you can then allocate jobs to everyone based on age and ability. Dr James Dobson's ministry 'Focus on the family' share some great information about age appropriate chores for children on their website. As a general rule I think it good if children have some regular daily and weekly chores but also are called on to help out randomly. So for example, children can be responsible for tasks such as making their beds every day, packing away toys, and generally clearing up after themselves as well as setting and clearing the table once or twice a week. On the next page is the family chores rota I currently use in my home. You may find it useful to know that my children are aged between 8 -17 years old and I had to actively teach them how to do their chores. For a long time I sounded like a broken record, frustrated with why mthey didn't carry out the tasks the way I wanted. It was Harold who emphasised the need to 'show' them exactly what to do and how to do it. Don't be afraid to train your children through demonstration then get them alongside you to ease them in. Don't assume they should know how to do anything. Once they have learned how to carry out their chores independently I still have a helpful checklist for them to go through to ensure they haven't missed anything. My husband typically studies and works a combined 40-50 hour week so isn't on hand very much but definitely helps out when needed. I think cooking is his favourite and to be honest, he is better at it than me! As I write this chapter it is the school Summer holidays but our current rota will change again in a few weeks as the autumn term begins.

Williams Family Chores Rota

Daily duties: Make Beds, Clear Bedroom floor (no clothes, toys or books), put belongings back in their place

Table/Dinner Duties

Set dining table for mealtimes: Putting out the cutlery, glasses, condiments etc. Clearing away after mealtimes, including wiping the table and sweeping the floor.

Day	Table duties	Prayer	Making K's breakfast
Monday	K	L	N
Tuesday	A	J	A
Wednesday	N	N	N
Thursday	J	A	A
Friday	L	K	N
Saturday	Mum	Dad	Mum
Sunday	Dad	Mum	Mum

Saturday Cleaning

L – Deep clean upper bathroom, Tidy bedroom and change bedlinen

J – Deep Clean the lower bathroom, Tidy bedroom, change bedlinen

N – Tidy the living room. Tidy Bedroom, Change bedlinen

A – Tidy the dining room. Tidy Bedroom, Change bedlinen

K – Empty dustbins (Living room, Focus room, bathroom and bedrooms

These chores are non-negotiable and everyone knows what their responsibilities are. I do tend to switch up the chores everyone does every four to six months just so they are able to develop a range of homemaking and cleaning skills. If you have younger children, consider switching it up a lot more frequently to keep them motivated. In addition to this rota I call on everyone randomly throughout the week to help pack away laundry, load and unload the dishwasher, assist with cooking and pack away groceries. It is worth saying that I do not pay any of my children to do household chores and I never will. I firmly believe that their responsibilities are simply part of what it takes to create and maintain the home they love. Their reward is the knowledge that they are wanted, needed and valuable to the functioning of a warm, loving and peaceful home. We are a family. We are a team.

Some useful tips!

1. For a sweet-smelling aroma around the house, try sprinkling cinnamon or some orange peel on a sheet of kitchen foil and placing in a warm oven. Keep on a low temperature. As it heats up, your home will soon be smelling yummy like you've been baking all afternoon!

2. When mopping hard floors, consider using washing powder in the water instead of traditional floor cleaners. It cuts through grime so easily.and leaves them squeaky clean.

3. Before using the hoover, dab a few cotton wool balls with your favourite essential oil and place in the bag/cylinder. Whilst using, the smell will permeate through your rooms.

4. Place half a lemon in the top draw of your dishwasher before running a cycle. It will smell great and leave dishes squeaky clean. Replace after two uses.

5. When dealing with grubby shirt collars, rub a small amount of washing up liquid on them before putting them to wash. Those dark necklines will disappear!

6. Baby wipes are great for quickly wiping down lots of things. Skirting boards, radiators and even leather sofas. This makes it an easy task to delegate to children.

7. Store sets of bedlinen inside one of the pillow cases. It will make finding everything you need much easier.

8. Invest in two door mats for the entrance of your home. One for inside the door and a more robust one for outside. This will mean that maximum dirt will be picked up from shoes before stepping onto your carpet or hard flooring.

9. When cooking strong smelling foods, close the kitchen door if you can. This will prevent the smell from travelling to the rest of the house which can sometimes be difficult to get rid of. If you have an open plan layout or studio home, open a window or two to aid the release of odours.

3
Managing routines and schedules

"When I had my first baby, I found it quite difficult to establish a routine which incorporated looking after my baby, going to work, doing housework and preparing meals. It was quite a stressful time as I was young and also getting to grips with the responsibility of raising my son and being a wife to my husband. I am an administrator and I decided to use my organisational skills to establish a routine of running the various tasks that I needed to do. This was done on A4 paper and it set out the task and the time (s) that the task had to be done by. I even put rest periods in it to ensure that I had time for myself. This schedule was invaluable to me when I went on to have my second baby and just slotted her into the equation. It's far easier to introduce a baby into your routine than the other way around. I used my schedule with all my children and passed on the principles to my own daughters."

– Sandra Edie

Setting up a Family Planner

~

The purpose of a family planner is to be able to see what every family member is doing on a daily, weekly or monthly basis at a glance. There are two main benefits for why I think every family should have some sort of planner:

To keep organised

A family planner is one of the easiest ways to manage everyday life and keep the whole family on the same page. If you are able to see an overview of everyone's activity, it can prevent clashes, overlapping and help you to plan ahead. The reality is that the activities of each family member can potentially affect others in the household either positively or negatively. Max may be the only one who needs to be at football practice on a Thursday evening but who will be dropping him off? Is Dad available? Will he need use of the shared car? How will thet fact that Dad will be out of the house for an amount of time affect the rest of the family? Or if Samantha is having friends round on Friday night will she need use of the family room or kitchen? What if Jenny has a college project to finish on the family computer which is kept in the living room? How will that impact everyone else? If you can see where everyone else will be ahead of time, then you're better equipped to work things out

To improve family relationships

Although the family is made up of a number of individual people, living completely independent lives can cause division. There should be a noticeable difference between the dynamics of a family to say that of flatmates. The main definition of a flatmate is "A person with whom one shares a flat". Flatmates have an agreement which will typically determine how bills will be split and similar arrangements in other areas. There need not be any love or care shared when it comes to these agreements. Flatmates can come and go as they please with no need for permission, accountability or consideration for the other party as long as it does not breach the terms of their agreement. Family is different. Though there is a level of agreement concerning the way the household is run, there is also relationship. There needs to be. If not for relationship, what then makes a family unique? Hopefully our family relationships are based on love which involves a greater degree of emotional investment and personal sacrifice than flatmates. A family planner is ammunition for enquiry, an invitation for conversation and opportunity for intimacy. This is because you are kept aware of what is happening in the life of your loved one on a regular basis.

Regardless of whether you purchase a family planner from a shop or make your own, there are some fundamental elements that I think it should have. For years I refused to go digital (I'm an old fashioned paper girl married to a tech head) and could manage quite efficiently with the planner in my diary. This was largely because the children were toddlers and I was in control of the running of most days. As they've grown, they have more of their own things going on. A digital calendar is much more accessible to everyone as it can be shared and viewed from

> *Keeping a Calendar is key. I write all of our family activities on the calendar. For example: where we are going, if the children are staying away from home, if I am working overtime, family events, birthday parties, Clubs etc.*
>
> *~ Danielle Edie*

multiple devices. Most smart phones come with some kind of time management and organisational tool built in. If not, there are many applications that can be installed either free or for a small fee. I would personally recommend having two planners that contain the same information. One can be displayed somewhere in the house where it can be glanced at by everyone and one digital that can be accessed wherever members are on the go.

On the next page are some examples of family planners that you could use to help get you started. The important thing is that it displays days and time slots with enough room for each family member's appointments. It can be for a week or month depending on how far in advance you need to see.

Family Planner – Example1   Week Beginning

	Mum	Dad	Max	Jenn	Samantha
Monday					
Tuesday					
Wednesday					
Thursday					
Friday					
Saturday					
Sunday					
Notes					

Week to view: Planner has a daily box for each family member. It may be helpful to add the time of each appointment in brackets.

In general, it is probably more efficient if you can include the actual time for each appointment e.g. *Football practice (5-6pm).* Start by inserting all **fixed activity**. So things like school, work, gym, church and regular commitments or extra-curricular activities.

Next, write in the **less regular** events. Some of these may not actually be attended but it is good to see them in the calendar anyway. These could be one-off or future things like birthday parties, meetings, medical appointments, school plays etc.

Family Planner – Example2   Week Beginning

	Mon		Tue		We		Thur		Fri		Sat		Sun	
	AM	PM	AM	PM	AM	PM	AM	PM	AM	PM	AM	PM	AM	PM
Mum														
Dad														
Max														
Jenn														
Sam														
Notes														

Week to view: Planner has two boxes per day, per family member. One for AM activity and the other for PM activity.

It may also be a good idea to purchase a yearly wall planner for the purpose of getting a broader overview of what is coming up in the year. Things like school holiday periods, planned vacations away, graduations, work experience or business trips, church retreats, self-development training and large social events like a milestone birthday party or retirement celebration. Whichever you choose to use, know that it must work for your family. If none of my suggestions found in this book help, find something else. It will be worth it. Finally, review the planner often because times and seasons change. Your organisational tools will need to adapt to suit the ever changing pace of life.

Family Planner – Example 3   Month _____

1	2	3	4	5	6
7	8	9	10	11	12
13	14	15	16	17	18
19	20	21	22	23	24
25	26	27	28	29	30
31	Notes				

Month to view: Planner has one box per day like a standard calendar. This is likely to work if you only have one or two people in the family or if there is very little change to your regular activity.

Daily Routines

~

The daily routine is just as important as having a family planner. In actual fact, without knowledge of the daily routine the family planner won't actually be as beneficial. Having a routine creates order, improves productivity and provides a structured environment which is particularly important for small children. Studies show that people who have a routine are:

1) value their time. A routine can help you to say no to many of the distractions of life that we encounter.
2) more relaxed (better prepared=less stressed)
3) more productive

Most people will generally have some type of a routine order of the day, which is comprised of a running order of things and a degree of flexibility at specific points during the day. Just like the planner, there will be things that will probably stay the same for the majority of the time. You get to decide what those things are but typically they will be things like waking and bedtimes, getting ready for the day, mealtimes, work and perhaps homework tasks. These times will usually be fixed, especially if you do a standard working week, have set hours that rarely change or structure things around school life. In our house, the morning and evening routines tend to stay the same.

This was what my morning and afternoon routines from 2012 looked like:

Morning

05:00	Wake Up, Hang up wet Laundry
05:15	Prayer and Read Bible
05:45	Get washed and dressed
06:00	Wake Family, Help Children to get ready
07:00	Breakfast
07:30	Clear away, wash dishes
07:45	Leave for School

This probably looks like I ran a very tight ship, and you're right, I did. We had moved to a new house and school was a 40-minute drive away so we had to leave out very early. At the time, the youngest was 4-years old and she did not like to travel so early but it had to be done. Her constant moaning and whining was stressful at the best of times but without a routine it would have been a disaster. At least this way she was able to get familiar with it so knew what to expect. If you have small children and no fixed routine, consider trying to implement one as I am sure you would find it beneficial and it can help children to co-operate a bit more. Between the hours of 09:00 and 14:30 there was a large degree of flexibility. You may have times during your day (or several days a week) that things can run much more loosely. That does not mean that you have free time as there will still be things to do but you may be able to choose how long you spend on each task and in what order you want to do them. It also means that you can shift things around to allow for the unexpected. For many days I had a list of things to get through but if an emergency came up or something unpredicted, I had a degree of flexibility to change things around. Years before when I was employed, the routine was less flexible during the day however the mornings and evenings probably looked similar. Whether you are employed for a set number of hours or work from home, routine will serve you well.

The evening looked like this:

Evening

14:30	Leave for the School run
16:00	Snacks, Bath/Wash the children
16:45	Help with homework
16:45	Clear away, straighten bedrooms
18:00	Dinner
19:00	Clear away, Wash dishes
19:30	Wind down, Bedtime stories
20:00	Children's Bedtimes
20:30	Iron tomorrow's clothing
	Programme Washing Machine

Again, pretty tight! After bedtime and ironing I had a few extra flexible hours that I probably filled with the things I fill them with now. Spending time with my husband, prepare something for the following day or catch up with writing my next book. Remember to re-evaluate your routines periodically. As much as my mornings and evenings are almost always set, they need changing on average every six months due to daily changes in life. The routine I had in

January 2016 has changed slightly due to one of my children who started secondary school this September. This may only be a slight change but will be necessary to ensure things are running as smoothly as possible. If a routine doesn't work for you, don't be afraid to change it! Allow older or more independent members of the family to come up with their own routines. They will know what works best for them as long as it doesn't change the family dynamic too much e.g. clashes with family times together.

Family meetings

~

Harold and I started to have family meetings with our children about ten years ago and have found them to be very useful. If you have never held one with your own family it may feel like a daunting idea, or you may have no idea where to begin. The easiest place to start will be by determining the need for the family meeting. It may be for a number of reasons, perhaps to inform family of a change that will affect everyone; to make an assessment of how family life is going; address a specific problem or concern; make a joint decision, or maybe you want to communicate some values or share your mission statement. In any case, the meeting should be an opportunity to discuss the kind of home you all want to see. It will allow everyone a chance to communicate their own experience of family life and how they feel things could improve. Whatever the purpose, I would advise you discuss with your spouse before involving any children.

Here are some basic guidelines if you would like to begin holding family meetings:

1. Decide on the date, time, duration and location e.g. Thursday 26th February, 6pm-6.30pm in the dining room.

2. Give family members prior notice - I would suggest at least a week. I like to create a notice of some kind by hand or on the computer which has all the relevant information, topics to be discussed and sometimes a few questions to get everyone thinking. You could get your children to do this in a creative way if you want.

3. Prepare for the meeting. Put together an agenda making photocopies if necessary. Buy in some light snacks so everyone can nibble along the way. A meeting over a full dinner has too many potential disruptions so I would not recommend that.

4. As the meeting begins, assign family members roles (this can be done before if you prefer). Make it clear who is chairing the meeting, taking minutes, handing out agendas etc. This is a great way of roping everyone

in and teaching children about the structure of meetings.

5. Explain the purpose for the meeting. Stick to an agenda but allow a certain degree of flexibility as something could come up that you did not foresee.

6. Allow everyone an opportunity to speak. You could try using clever open questions to encourage quieter members to share.

7. Summarise at the end, highlighting any action points to be done (including a deadline). Display the action points in a place where they can be reviewed easily.

8. Close the meeting thanking everyone for their participation and remind them that you are a team.

Tips for making the most of meetings

- Feel free to *make meetings fun*, you want to make sure they are a positive experience. You could start with a lively icebreaker or a sing song. Even if you discuss a difficult subject, the meeting need not leave a negative taste in anyone's mouth.

- Don't be afraid to use visuals to help illustrate any important points. This could be pictures, demonstrations or a short video clip. Getting family members to engage in a role play can be very powerful aswell.

- Make sure you allow everyone ample time to share their views. It is good to get children's considerations as they often highlight things adults forget or overlook. Doing this means that everyone will feel valued.

- If necessary, come up with a strategy on how you will manage if people talk over one another. You may want to set up some kind of ground rules beforehand or have an object that is held by the person who is talking. Be creative!

- Store minutes in a designated folder or file for easy access. You may choose to have summarised bullet points displayed openly as reminders.

As you develop the habit of holding family meetings it will become a normal part of family life and over time be some of the most productive times for you all.

4

Administration and household accounts

Family Admin! What is that?

~

Nowadays, you can have paperless everything. You can have your bills, bank statements, contracts, warranty's and insurance policies in a digital format. Increasingly schools and nurseries communicate to parents using a blog or website, send text messages to phones or on digital platforms like ParentMail. As time speeds on, paper appears to be becoming less used. Some of us however (remember I mentioned that I am an old fashioned paper girl) continue to keep hard copies of everything. This can take up a huge amount of space but I simply seem to process things better when I have it in a tangible form. A large part of managing a home involves staying on top of the paperwork and to be honest, even if the majority of your files are digital, you will need to have some kind of system for storing these important documents. I call this family admin.

Family admin can include:

- Creating and maintaining routines and schedules
- Household bills
- Dealing with incoming and outgoing mail

- Meal Planning and Grocery shopping
- Medical Documents and Appointments
- School Letters and Reports
- Financial Management
- Receipts, Warranties and Insurance Policies
- Tax and Employment Documents
- Voting information
- Filing
- Any other household system

If you are going to prevent paying bills late, missing appointments or forgetting to renew the home contents insurance, you must make deliberate actions to avoid doing so. As with much of the content of this book, you will have to find out what systems work best for you. If like me, you prefer to have everything on paper then having a large binder for each category is probably the easiest option. If you have a lot of documentation, then investing in a filing cabinet would be more favourable. I would actually recommend everyone purchase at least a small filing cabinet because there are some things such as birth certificates for example that just aren't available digitally. In addition, there may be some older documents that you do not want to throw away and so you will need somewhere to store them.

Although it is all well and good having filing systems in place, they will be no good if you never refer to them. It is wise to have a simple "inbox" or "in-tray" for things that you need to action. Once they have been completed then you can file them away. To prevent having a mammoth-sized in-tray be diligent to check through it several times a week. A friend of mine checks hers every single day. You may only need to check once a week but the key is to do so regularly. I think once a week is the ideal minimum. Things that can be done in less than five minutes, determine to do straight away. Everything else will need to be factored into your schedule for the week. Thinking you will get around to it without deliberately making time is risky business. Trust me. I have learnt this the hard way! I have been guilty on many an occasion of letting the in-tray grow to the size of Mount Everest!

For the things that need managing infrequently (like an annual car insurance) you could set digital reminders for yourself or write them in on a yearly planner. Most companies will contact you when the end of your policy is soon due for renewal. It is in the company's best interest to do this because they want your business. If they do not automatically prompt you, you may need to proactively make contact.

'To do' lists can be a great way to keep on top of things. I do them weekly and then split that weekly list into day tasks. It can be incredibly rewarding when you see your list at the end of the day and everything is ticked off (or has a big fat line drawn through it). So by now you can probably see that when it comes to managing your home effectively, you will need to have a broad overview of what is happening and upcoming (the family planner, chores rota) but also need things in place to manage the finer details (daily routines, systems and to-do's).

A lot of work goes into keeping on top of things and the reality is that there will be busy seasons when it is near impossible to do so. These tips are not intended to hold you to ransom but instead make life more productive. Proactivity is always favoured over reactivity. With the right systems for the needs of your household, hopefully you'll be freed up to do more of what you love.

Home finances - The basics

~

Money stress can be one of the biggest causes of contention in the home so despite not being an expert on the subject, I felt it was very important to add this chapter. In the following few pages I will simply be sharing some of my own tips that will help you to manage the money that makes its way through your home. There is always much room to grow in this area because whether we have little or lots, we are stewards of our money. How we use it is very important if we are to live a life that is thriving and it can work for or against us depending on how well we steward it. In order to do this, it may be worth looking into what your money language is. A money language essentially controls how you see and use money to express love. Financial Psychologist Kenneth Doyle outlines four of them. I have included them below:

Driver – Money means success. A driver says I love you" by buying things and showing you through material objects you are important to them. Obviously, taken too far this can become materialistic and non-relational.

Analytical – Money means security. Analytics say "I love you" through saving and planning for the future. Taken too far they can become miserable, no fun and controlling. They can also communicate more value for money than people.

Amiable - Money means love. An amiable says "I love you" by sharing and giving. Without balance and wisdom, an amiable can be impulsive and unprepared for the future.

Expressive - Money means acceptance. Expressives say "I love you" by buying, showing and sharing. Taken too far, expressives use money the way some people use alcohol—to deal with pain and anxiety in a wrong manner.

Knowing which money language you have will be a great place to start when understanding how to handle your money.

We have a responsibility to manage our money well because essentially, it represents our life. Whether we work part-time hours, do a 9-5 office job or own a business, most of us obtain our money in exchange for our *time*. In exchange for our *life*.

The time we spend working, we will never ever get back so the last thing we ought to do is squander it. We all have goals and dreams for our money even if we do not consciously consider what they are. Some of us focus on using our money to party on the weekend, going on shopping sprees or treating ourselves and others to a variety of luxuries. Others may pay more attention to savings and investments, making ends-meet or sowing into a business. Knowing what your goals are for your money is a great place to start if you want to begin to get a handle on money management. Seek financial advice from a professional if you need help, especially if you have debt. "What's your financial Gameplan?" by Neala Okuromade is a fantastic book to start the process.

If you live with a spouse or partner, ensure there is agreement regarding how money will be managed. This will lend to a calmer home with less strife. My husband and I agree that our household income is one despite the fact that we both earn money from several different streams. So there is no such thing as 'my money' and 'his money' despite the fact we both make an income. There is one pot and together we decide what goes where. I know of some arrangements where couples go halves on everything or where the husband may pay the mortgage and utilities and the wife pays for the groceries, children's activities, clothing etc. Whatever arrangement you decide to have, remember that there must be agreement and that you are a team!

3 Basic principles to manage money well

Regular monitoring of your income and expenditure

You will never be able to handle money well if you have no idea how much you even have to work with. At the very least we have a responsibility to know how much we have coming in and how much we need to pay out on a regular basis. Our management of what we have left after paying our essential bills is what can give us options or create problems. The easiest way to do this may be to make an income and outgoings list (see diagram). Once you've done this, you'll be able to see whether you are even able to cover your basic needs and if you have any surplus.

Monthly Income		Monthly Outgoings	
Wages	£1500	Rent	£800
Child Benefit	£82.80	Council Tax	£60
		Gas	£25
Total	**£1582.80**	Electricity	£35
		Groceries and Toiletries	£40
		Mobile Phone Contract	£35
		Travel Card	£102.20
		Savings	£50
		Total	**£1147.20**
Income minus Outgoings =		**£435.60**	

Example of income and outgoings

Although this is not a realistic view of everything one may need to pay on a monthly basis, it gives us a general overview of a financial situation. We are provided with a starting point for making our money work for us instead of the other way around. In addition, it is wise to go through bank statements on a regular basis, especially if you have direct debits and use a debit card for purchases. You can opt to use online banking to check in on your balance daily or weekly.

Have a budget that you stick to

I love budgeting because it has so many benefits. For starters, it gives you much greater control over what happens to your money. How many of us have received a sum of money only to have no clue of what we ended up spending it on? Most of us I suspect. Budgeting means that you intentionally decide how your money will be spent *before* you even have it. It will give you much greater awareness of your financial situation, meaning a greater chance of foreseeing the likelihood of problems occurring. You can write a standard budget by hand, starting with what must be paid and adding everything else. You will be able to distinguish between what is essential and what is not, then can adjust accordingly. Once you have set your budget, don't forget that it then needs to be upheld and managed. Refer to it often, ensuring you work out how much you are able to spend on lunch every day for example or how many cups of coffee you can get from Starbucks in a given month.

Store financial information

Not being able to find a financial document when you need it is nothing less than frustrating. Stacks of unopened bills never helped anyone so decide on how you are going to store your financial records reliably. This includes bank statements, bills, contracts, credit card statements, employment and tax information, trust funds, savings accounts, receipts and anything else money related. A financial folder can be good for storing all the things that have yet to be dealt with and a filing system for storing things you'll need to reference. Having a system to your storing financial documents is essential whether you hold physical or digital copies of everything. If your bills and statements are emailed to you, make sure you organise your email folders in such a way that you can quickly access if you need to. I would also recommend downloading copies to your device as an extra backup. Remember to do thorough financial maintenance, destroying old documents (keep for at least five years) every now and again to keep things in order.

Helping with Homework

~

Should you choose to send your child to mainstream school (in the UK children start primary school between the age of four and five years old) sometimes it can be challenging to keep on top of their homework assignments. Times of study can end up being a very stressful time for both parent and child. Whether you child loves or hates homework, brings home loads or very little, try using these tips to help develop good study habits. It is worth saying that a school is not solely responsible for educating your child. As a parent you must take the reins when it comes to ensuring they are learning. Sometimes this may mean that home or flexi-schooling may be more beneficial. If you have never heard of flexi-schooling it is a combination of attending mainstream school for a set amount of days per week and home-schooling the rest of the time. This chapter is geared towards parents of children who attend mainstream school on a fulltime basis although the tips can be applied by anyone.

Read to and with your child

Reading to your child has many benefits but most of all they learn that reading can be enjoyable. When we read a range of text types, add funny voices and use lots of expression we make the experience fun and inviting. As a result, our children gain essential listening and thinking skills, learn to use their imaginations, develop concentration and become avid readers. Reading builds up language skills and vocabulary and has been proven to increase IQ. So encourage them to read independently and out loud to you regularly. To be honest, whatever you choose to read together doesn't matter so much but try to introduce a variety. That being said, if your child finds Shakespeare utterly boring, opt for something that interests them. Football, animals, shopping, whatever. Remember that books aren't the only things that contain words. Consider comics, newspapers and magazines, e-books and even billboards, posters or road signs.

Get clued up

Even very young children can bring home homework that feels beyond us. For most parents it has probably been a while since we were in primary education and methods may have changed. Make it your responsibility to become familiar with the basics of the national curriculum. One of the easiest ways to stay informed is by simply talking to your child's class teacher. Ask for an explanation of basic maths strategies or writing methods to use with your child so that they remain consistent with what is done at school. This way our children will be encouraged when what is being taught in both places is the same.

Have a homework routine
Where possible, factor in some regular time during the week for focussed learning and homework. Try to choose an optimal time when you and your child are relaxed and feeling positive. About 45 minutes to an hour after school works in my house bearing in mind that my youngest is eight. Have a designated place to work like the dining room table, study room if you have one or even a desk in the bedroom. In the Summer months, homework can even be done outside in the sun! You could try creating a structured timetable which includes specific topics e.g. phonics, spellings, timestables We almost always start with 10-15 minutes of reading (20-30 minutes for the juniors) then move on to whatever homework the class teacher has set (this usually is no longer

than 30 minutes). If none has been set, we may do some other home study that will usually link to a topic at school. Have a five-minute break if necessary.

Physically stay to support them

Regardless of our children's ability, our presence can help to form a positive association with homework. By sitting down with them we can gain a greater understanding of their strengths and weaknesses. We can also be on hand to help if needed. If your child is quite confident or gets nervous with you peering over their shoulder, try setting up a spot on a part of the table nearby and get on with some paperwork yourself. I will often complete some household or business admin, mark coursework, write a blog post or even enter in diary dates. Whatever you do, try not to completely disappear and focus somewhere else.

Observe how your child learns best

Not all children find sitting down at a desk to do a task interesting. In actual fact, studies show that most children do not learn best in this way alone. As much as 50% of learners are Kinaesthetic. This means that they learn best by *doing* as opposed to simply hearing or seeing information. Your child may prefer to move around, listen to music or talk things through. Become familiar with factors that help your child to focus. Some children can only concentrate for a few minutes at a time so regular breaks can help them stay on task. When teaching my children the books of the Bible, my husband and I used a song which was far more effective than other memory methods. Don't be afraid to include a variety of alternatives if it has a positive effect on your child's learning. Use media clips, the internet, educational board games and creative resources. Sometimes listening to sounds of nature or very soft music can help my children to focus on homework.

Additional tips:

- Try to avoid setting written tasks as consequences for negative behaviour. This may build a negative association to homework and assignments

- If either you or your child are getting angry or frustrated, it may be wise to take a break and revisit the task. In some cases, I have abandoned it altogether and tried again another day.

- As children get older be careful not to remove yourself from being a place of support. Although young people may have grown in understanding (my teens know more about academics than me in some respects) and developed independent study techniques make a point to still be on hand if necessary. Ask them about what they are studying. What do they find easy or enjoyable? What is a bit more of a challenge at the moment? Help them set a few healthy achievable goals. Communicate your healthy expectation of them to try their best. Be careful not to impose your personal dreams and desires as children may have difficulty living up to those. Let them be themselves but push enough for them to know you are their biggest cheerleader.

A word about Computers

In this digital age, homework is increasingly being set on websites meaning it needs to be completed on a computer.

This can be a challenge if a) you don't own a computer and b) if you have more than one child. With seven of us in our household we have reached the stage where we could all do with a laptop each! Both my husband and I do a lot of work on our business using the internet, we manage and fulfil church responsibilities and manage household admin etc. In the evenings when our children are home, some days they have all been given homework needed to be completed on the computer! This has become somewhat of a challenge. If we were all to take turns there still wouldn't be enough time for everyone to finish their assignments!

If like us, your family share devices or have a challenge that means it is hard to access a computer, have a chat with the class teacher about it. Ask if they could substitute the work with written sheets instead or extend the deadline to give you a little more time.

Remember! Academic achievements aren't everything! Many children and young adults are under a tremendous amount of pressure to perform well, remember to celebrate efforts, not only grades.

5

Cooking and health management

Health Education

~

Not long ago my eight-year-old told me something that concerned me slightly. She said "Mum did you know that there are so many of my friends that didn't know that chips come from potatoes!" I hadn't deeply considered how important health education is for everyone, especially the future generations. I also felt quite ignorant about the number of children that wouldn't have a health education purely because their parent or guardian hadn't taught them anything. Raising children who have no knowledge or understanding of where our food comes from or a healthy diet is an injustice to the future generations. If we are not deliberate about investing this wealth into our children, they may not learn what is paramount for sustained health and strength into their adult years. Fruit and veg aren't optional in my house. Though not everyone likes that rule all the time, they are aware that it exists and is adhered to by everyone. I remember when my children were all toddlers and complaints about broccoli on the dinner plate were common. I made a very conscious decision to clear up any ambiguity about the status of vegetables in our house by simply telling the children that there will be vegetables at every meal. No amount of moaning or complaints would change that because health is important. One of my sons does not like mushrooms. I cook them anyway. Aubergine, Kale and Sweet potatoes are others that have sparked a protest, however they still appear, sometimes hidden but often not. Teaching children that food can be enjoyed but should also be healthy is to equip them with life wealth.

Out of desperation some parents choose to "hide" vegetables by blending them into meals or disguising them and although we must do everything we can to ensure our children get adequate nutrition, I encourage parents not to do this with every vegetable. Children need to get used to seeing vegetables, become familiar with their natural look, taste and texture. Eventually they will be presented with normal looking fruit and veg and if it is completely alien to them, all the best trying to get them to embrace them. Here are some of my top tips when it comes to making sure our children are clued up.

Be a role model

There is nothing more powerful than being a role model to your children. They are more likely to do what you do than do what you say. If you regularly encourage them to eat your home cooked meal but then order takeaway for yourself, they will come to the conclusion that your advice is flawed. You want them to follow your example. As they say, talk is cheap.

Limit Sweets and Junk food

Reduce the amount of sugar and junk foods you consume as a family. If you eat them regularly this may be tricky. I would recommend reducing the amount by a third to begin with and take the time to learn about healthier alternatives. So if you visit fast food outlets six days a week, reduce it to four days and cook the rest of the time. Almost ten years ago I decided that the children were eating too many sweets. I would collect them from school and be horrified to discover that another friend had celebrated a birthday and given out party bags to everyone. It was too often for me and so I declared a 'sweetie day'. Fridays in our house is sweetie day. So that means that no one buys or eats sweets on the other six days of the week with the exception of a special event on the weekend. So if someone else buys sweets for my children and it isn't Friday, they don't get eaten. They are stored away until Friday. Of course, there have been times when this rule has been broken but it is the general consensus. Consider whether you could implement a sweetie day.

Talk about food

Children like to understand the 'why' behind everything so talk to them about the relationship between eating certain foods and its effect on the body. If they have a deeper understanding of the benefits of healthy eating, they are more likely to understand why you insist they eat their broccoli. This does become easier as they grow up but if you say that eating a healthy breakfast helps them to concentrate on their school work or spinach will mean they get sick less often, in time they will begin to understand. You could display food education visuals around the kitchen or dining area. I have a set of place mats that have a picture of a healthy plate of food on. It includes labels of what is a carbohydrate, protein, vegetable and portion sizes. I also have a chart on the kitchen wall that has information about seasonal fruit and veg. So if I have strawberries in the fridge during the Autumn months, the children know that they've been imported.

Stay Active

Do something, anything that will get the whole family moving! It doesn't have to be that you plan tailored workouts for everyone. If you drive, you could decide on some places that you refuse to take the car and have everyone walk instead. Dance around the house, play football in the park, go bike riding or buy a trampoline for the garden. Either way, stay active and deliberately build this in your children. Have them doing extra-curricular activities that are not only good for their academic success but also for their health. Get outside and breathe in the fresh air, visit the park, go for walks and enjoy it!

So far in this chapter, there has been an emphasis on food but we must understand that there are some other things that contribute to being healthy.

Sleep

Do not underestimate the importance of adequate sleep. So many of us habitually burn the midnight oil to our detriment. I understand that it often feels as though we do not have enough hours in the day but we literally reduce the amount of time we have left to live by failing to sleep enough. It is during our times of sleep that our body gets an opportunity to *recover*. This is just as, if not more important for children. Sleeping actually promotes healthy growth, body and brain function. Establish some sort of bedtime routine for everyone, including yourself that involves winding down instead of slumping into bed exhausted every night. Find out whether your child is getting enough sleep by checking out the NHS website.

Emotional wellbeing

Mental and emotional health is a massive factor in the overall quality of your life. A person's ability to overcome adversity and challenges can be the difference between success and failure. There are several things that go into ensuring that we are healthy emotionally, some we can control and others that we cannot. For children, their initial attachment and continued relationship with parents plays an important role.

Children who have a positive relationship with their parents statistically feel more secure and have a stronger self-esteem. Having extended family support either from grandparents or other relatives is also a benefit. For many of us, the experiences of receiving love, being able to problem solve and express ourselves creatively has an impact on how we feel about ourselves. Stress isn't good for anyone, and left unaddressed can spiral into depression or worse. Ask yourself some probing questions regularly that will give you an idea of whether you are actually okay. Questions like, 'Am I happy? If not, why not?'. Do I feel fulfilled in my life? How am I really? Do I hold any grudges against anyone? Am I moody all the time? These kinds of questions will help you to identify where you are emotionally and give you the ammunition you need to go about addressing any issues. Take some time out to rest and recuperate if you are feeling overwhelmed. Be still, pray and shut off all outside distractions if you need to.

Meal Planning

~

Why Meal Plan?

I would definitely recommend Meal planning as it saves both time and money. It also increases your awareness of what the family are eating and how much of a healthy, varied diet every person is consuming. Planning ahead can reduce levels of stress that frequently surround mealtimes and less food is likely to be wasted. Like lots of children, mine are often asking me what is for dinner. By displaying a meal plan on my kitchen wall for all to see, this questioning often reduces. Additionally, if your children know what is on the menu in advance they will be less surprised when their least favourite vegetable appears

*When I was expecting with my eldest child (now 9 yrs old), I decided to read lots of books on parenting and cooking for children. I happened to come across Annabel Karmel's **Super foods for Babies and Children**. This book was amazing as it took the worry out of weaning my baby. Its nutritional meals are so simple and easy to follow. My 4 children loved all the recipes and so I use it regularly. You must have it!"*
~ **Aida Ghebretensae**

on their plate on Thursday night. There are many ways to meal plan and I would recommend exploring methods then adapting to suit the needs of your family.

Meal Planning - Cons

Meal Planning definitely involves effort and initially will seem very time consuming. The best advice I could offer for that is to keep at it, it becomes easier! Meal planning can prove to be completely pointless if and when you have unexpected visitors. Yes, people should really let you know if they are going to visit, particularly if they are expecting food but it doesn't always go like that. I have found myself with unexpected visitors on several occasions around dinner time and there is nothing worse than not having enough food cooked to feed everyone! Things don't always go according to plan!

Meal Planning - How to with Ten Steps

I have included the basic method I use for weekly meal planning the dinners only. Feel free to tweak it to suit you and the needs of your family.

1. Create a folder (either physical or digital) to keep all meal planning info in - Meal ideas, menus, shopping lists and receipts etc.

2. Set yourself a realistic grocery budget - This can be per week or month depending on how long you want to meal plan for. Your grocery budget will somewhat determine the meals you can and cannot have i.e. there is no point putting down an expensive food item on the menu if the cost is way above your means

3. Write out a list of all regular and staple items that you may need - These are the things you know you are likely to need on a weekly basis i.e. milk, butter, eggs bread or things you always keep supplies of like flour, herbs or baking ingredients

4. Write an estimated cost rounded up to the nearest 50p next to each staple item based on the quantity you will need - If half a dozen eggs costs £1.99 and you know you go through a dozen then you will need to assign £4.00 for that item

5. Total up the cost of all staple items needed and deduct this amount from your set budget

---

Grocery Budget = £100

    Staple items

      Milk £5.00   Grocery Budget – Staple items

      Bread £2.00   = Remaining budget available

      Cereal £5.00

      Honey £400   £100.00-£20.00 = **£80.00**

      Eggs £4.00

  Total = £20.00

---

6. Decide what meals you would like to eat for the next week (or other chosen time frame). You could use recipe books, online recipes, known favourites and recommendations from friends or family. YouTube has lots of quick and easy recipe channels to learn from.

Try to keep it varied, but note that the more varied the menu, the greater the cost is likely to be.

7. Write down a list of ingredients needed to make your chosen meals

8. Any ingredients that you already have in the house or have included on your staples list need not be written again

9. Assign each ingredient an estimated cost rounded up to the nearest 50p

10. Total up the cost of items ensuring it falls within your set budget. If it is over you will need to consider leaving out some items or opting for more cost effective choices.

Cost of staple items + Meal ingredients

=

<u>Total grocery budget to spend</u>

Once you have completed these steps you can take your list to the store and grab only the items written down (although I do sometimes add a few sneaky extras if the budget allows). Display the menu in your dining room or kitchen for family members to view.

Grocery Shopping Tips

~

Shopping for groceries need not be an negative experience but in order for things to be as stress free as possible, it does require some planning. However frequently you replenish your kitchen, here are my top tips for preparing and executing shopping for groceries. Some of the tips included in the previous chapter are skimmed over in the paragraphs ahead.

Do an inventory

Before you even head out to the shops I would recommend having a look around your kitchen to see what supplies you already have in stock. It's amazing how many times I have bought flour or some other item only to find it in abundance when packing it away. Depending on sell by dates, this could mean that the product gets wasted and in addition, you have spent money that simply could've gone elsewhere. Make a note on a piece of paper of the things you already have in stock so you remember they need not be added to your shopping basket.

Have a flexible budget

Set an initial overall budget. The average weekly spend for a family of four in the UK in 2014 was £58.50 (Office of National statistics, 2014). Ensure that you cut your coat according to size and set a budget that will adequately feed your family without bursting your pockets. If this is difficult you may need to rethink how you feed everyone, opting for more low cost meals. When deciding on the amount for your budget I would suggest adding a few extra pounds to allow for some flexibility. This will help to deal with price increases or and allow you to take advantage of an unexpected offer that you might find.

Make a list

Once the budget is set you can go ahead and make a grocery list. Be sure to make a list *every* time you go grocery shopping even if you are only popping out for a handful of items. This will help you to not deviate from the things you need and you are more likely to avoid wasting money. It will also ensure that you do not forget anything. Assign each item a realistic budget based on current prices, you could even use past receipts to help you with this. For the sake of flexibility round each itemised budget up to the nearest fifty pence. I am a firm believer in frugality and if you desire to steward your money well I would advocate doing this. The total of all your items should come in at or under the budget you have already set. If it does not, you will need to shift things around or remove some items entirely.

Visit the supermarket at quieter times

Supermarkets are busy most of the times these days but if braving them at peak times is too overwhelming for you I would suggest going at less busy times. I have found this to generally be midweek either first thing in the morning or later at night. Make the most of supermarkets that are open 24 hours or that shut very late. You will find that there are less people around (including children) thus making your trip faster and more peaceful. One of the down sides of shopping at these times is that you may find a lot more staff restocking shelves. I don't really like this as I feel they are in my way but prefer to deal with that over packed aisles and long queues. Try to ensure you have eaten before going shopping as you'll only end up buying more food.

Invest in a trolley token and reusable carrier bags

There is something very frustrating about needing loose change for a parking meter or in this case the trolley in the supermarket when you don't have any! You are then faced with the task of having to find some, either by going into the store to buy something or asking other shoppers. Both options can be very frustrating and cost us time so to avoid this dilemma invest in a trolley token. These can be purchased at a very small price of a pound or two and can be used again and again. Trolley tokens are the same size, shape and weight as a £1 coin which are often required to be inserted into a trolley you intend to use for your groceries. I buy two, one to keep in the car and the other on my keys which are kept in my purse.

In October 2015, the UK Government introduced a new law that obliges all large retailers to charge 5p for every single use carrier bag. This was in a bid to reduce the number of single use carrier bags and cut down on the damage they cause to our environment. Because of this I would recommend purchasing several stronger 'bags for life' and bringing them along to each shopping trip. Consider using a rucksack to carry heavier items such as cans or bottled water. You could also use a shopping trolley for £10-£20 that can be purchased from most major home retail stores.

Familiarise yourself with the store layout

We ideally want to be in and out of the store as quickly and efficiently as possible. This can be difficult at the best of times but if we are familiar with the layout it may just save us more time. There are certain aisles that I very rarely visit and so avoid altogether. If I don't need any wine or fizzy drinks (they are hardly ever on my list) then there is absolutely no point me visiting these areas. If you order your shopping list according to the layout of the store this should be easily done but in the event of you needing to grab something you forgot to add or hadn't planned, you can quickly locate it.

Check prices against offers

Just because you have spotted a special offer that looks great doesn't mean that it actually is. Remember supermarkets still make huge amounts of profit and getting you to spend more is one of their primary goals.

Example

A single 2kg bag of rice retails at £3.39

An offer states

"2 bags of 2kg basmati rice for £6.00 Saving £0.78p"

When you look at the 4kg bag it retails at £5.89.

Although you only save 11p, it makes more sense to go with the 4kg bag as this saves you money and gives you the same 4kg of rice.

So an offer isn't always saving you money. Check them out to be sure.

Get children involved

For those of us that have children, most of us would probably say that we would rather shop for groceries without them. This is because they tend to ask for the 'million' things they encounter along the way. It is also much easier to cart a trolley around and buy what we need without the added hassle of having to keep our eyes on a child or two. But for those times when they have to tag along, the biggest piece of advice I would give you is to get them involved. Even the youngest of children can help to load things into the trolley.

Get older children to help by crossing items off a list, using a calculator to monitor the budget, weigh produce and help to pack once you've paid. Not only will they feel useful but they are also learning how to shop for groceries efficiently themselves.

Visiting different stores

Don't feel like you have to get everything under one roof! There are so many different shops at our disposal, particularly in city centres and many of them are within walking distance of one another. The larger supermarkets don't always offer the best deal so don't be afraid to shop around. It may be wise to walk a few minutes up the road in order to save a few pounds. Recently my husband and I were on the lookout for some strong kitchen towels. In the first shop which was a well-known chain store sold a large roll for £2.69 and just two doors down we found the same jumbo roll for £1! That's a difference of £1.69 for an extra thirty seconds walk! Sometimes the price difference costs more than the fuel you use to travel ten minutes in the car.

Other ways to save money

- If you decide to frequent more than one shop, ensure you mark on your list which items are coming from which store.

- If driving, ensure there is parking available and check whether it is paid or not. Remember to be aware that most supermarkets offer free parking for only a few hours. Make sure you move your car within the given timeframe to avoid hefty parking fines.

- Eat before leaving home so you don't get tempted to buy food on the go.

- Leave unused debit or credit cards at home. This will help you to stick to your budget and enable you to resist the urge to buy unneeded extras.

- Branded items don't always taste better. Do your research by trying a new product every now and again, you just might be surprised how much money you save without compromising on taste.

A few quick recipes

~

'Almost' Homemade Pizza

Ingredients

Pizza Dough (ready-made)

Can of chopped or plum tomatoes

Dash of Balsamic Vinegar

½ tsp Paprika

1 tsp Dried herbs

A selection of chosen toppings

Cheese (Optional)

Salt and Pepper to Taste

Remove the pizza dough from the fridge, roll out and leave at room temperature for ten minutes. Meanwhile, chop up or slice all your chosen toppings. Next, put the tomatoes, vinegar, herbs, paprika, salt and pepper into a blender or food processor. Blend until smooth. Spread tomato sauce onto your Pizza base (it may look thin at this stage but is perfectly normal). Distribute toppings evenly onto the tomato base then top with cheese (optional). Bake in the oven at 200 degrees Celsius for approximately 15-20 minutes or according to the packet instructions. Serve with a green salad and garlic bread.

Peanut Butter Noodles

Ingredients

2x 375g Egg or Rice Noodles

1 large Courgette (spiralized or cut into thin strips)

1 ½ cups of Vegetable stock

4 large tbls of Whole Grain Peanut Butter

2 Jumbo Spring Onions

1 large Sweet Bell Pepper

Salt and pepper to taste

Garlic (optional)

Cook the noodles according to the instructions given on the packet. Meanwhile, deseed and chop the sweet bell pepper into thin strips, slice the spring onions and garlic. Put the vegetables into a large pot or frying pan with a few tablespoons of water. Cook the peppers, onions and garlic for 2-3 minutes stirring frequently to avoid sticking. Add an additional few tablespoons of water if needed. Once the vegetables have softened, add 1 ½ cups of vegetable stock and bring to the boil. Add peanut butter, salt and pepper to the mixture and stir well. Simmer for a further few minutes then turn off the heat. Drain the noodles and stir into the peanut sauce. Add the spiralized courgette to the mix and serve

Steamed Salmon with Cabbage

Ingredients needed

1 tbls of coconut oil

4 Salmon filets (fresh or frozen)

1 large white onion chopped

3 medium tomatoes chopped

Two cups of any cabbage, chopped (I like to use savoy)

Salt and black pepper to taste

A dash of Encona Hot pepper sauce

Steam Salmon gently in a tiered steamer pan or pot with a little water. Leave to cook for 10 minutes. Once cooked, remove from the pan and flake into a bowl. Season with a little salt and pepper. Lightly fry the onions in oil for 2-3 minutes or until translucent. Add tomatoes to the pan, cover and simmer for further 2-3 minutes. Season well. Add the flaked Salmon filets and stir into tomatoes and onions. Pour half a cup of water into the pan and add a dash of hot pepper sauce. Add chopped cabbage, turn down the heat, cover and allow to simmer for 5 minutes or until cabbage is cooked through. Serve with yam or sweet potatoes.

One pot Pasta with Pesto

Ingredients

Dried Pasta shapes of your choice

1-2 Jars of Green or Red Pesto

Salt to taste

Any leftover veg you can find in your fridge.

Bring a large pan of water to the boil. Rinse pasta in cold water, drain then add to the water. Cook pasta on a medium heat for the recommend time on the packaging. Lightly fry any leftover vegetables you want to use and set aside. Once the pasta is cooked, drain and place in a large bowl, adding the vegetables. Pour in two jars of a pesto of your choice and mix well. You could try adding olives to give a zingy taste. Serve immediately

6
Repairs and household developments

A Yearly Review and planning ahead

~

A yearly review is something that my husband and I have only really begun to embrace in the last few years but are passionate about continuing to develop it. Most of us do a level of evaluation at least on a yearly basis. We may ask ourselves "What did I achieve?" or "How have I improved?" If you have developed a habit of setting goals, then you probably review these too. According to the Oxford English Dictionary one definition of the word Review is:

*To **assess** (something) formally with the intention of* ***instituting change if necessary***

So we review something in order to know whether the state of it has changed (either for better or for worse) and find out if all is as it should be. We then can decide whether anything needs adjusting in order for a milestone to be reached or to ensure continued success. A good time to do a review is towards the end of the year, so you have enough time to decide what may need to change. As with any area of our life, it is good to set some kind of goals for our home and how we manage it. I would recommend doing a review several times throughout the year to stay focussed but if you are very new to the process, follow these steps to do a basic yearly review.

Take stock of the last twelve months

To take stock simply means *to think about and make an overall assessment of a thing.* Do this with the last year. Ponder on the things you have done and events that have happened, then acknowledge them. Perhaps you planned to give your home some much needed re-decoration but it didn't happen due to a lack of finances. Ask yourself why this happened. Did you manage your resources effectively? Could you have completed works in one area but didn't? Why not? Did you have a plan on how you were going to get the jobs done? Reflect on why these things may not have happened and ask yourself what can you learn from them. Use your conclusions to decide what you want to be different next year.

Set some household management goals for the coming year

Decide what you want to happen in the year ahead. Do you want the ambiance in your home to be more peaceful this year? Do you want the children to bicker less? Do you need to improve the relationship with your spouse? Maybe that creaky door finally needs fixing? Does the wardrobe that has been falling apart need replacing? Are there piles of paperwork everywhere? Whatever you want to change, note it down. It may be particularly useful to do this in the form of a spider diagram so you can get everything out and see it clearly.

Acknowledge major upcoming events and milestones

When my husband and I do this we also write down any significant events that are taking place. Usually these are things that we know could and will change the way we do life somewhat, or that mark the beginning or end of a season. So for example, last year we noted that our eldest woule be turning sixteen, leaves secondary school and starts A-levels. This year we noted that our third son will sit his SATS tests and begin secondary school. If we have these things on our radar it will help us to adjust more quickly and plan ahead.

Planning ahead

Example of how you could do a Spider diagram

Include household projects

No household improvement is too big or small to include in your review. Make a note of everything from replacing lightbulbs to refurbishments. You could ask yourself what would be the benefits of investing in home developments. Do you want it to be more aesthetically pleasing in order to motivate you or bring a sense of tranquillity? Will you be able to function much better if you create a laundry space? When you break down what needs to be done, even if only in a list form it suddenly becomes more achievable. You may not have £300 to redecorate and re-furnish your bedroom but you could have £50 to replace the curtains. If this small improvement will help you to love your home more then it may just be worth it.

Consider large purchases

Look forward and try to predict what major purchases you may need to make. How likely is it that you'll need to replace your car this coming year? Does the lease on your flat end? Are you planning a family holiday or large celebration? Will your 10-year old washer/dryer last another 12 months? Perhaps one of your children have a school journey that will cost a few hundred pounds? Again this is good to know in order for you to prepare accordingly. Equally, if you know there is no way you will have the money, you can put something in place which will generate the income.

Relationship and Family Goals

Don't forget to highlight areas you want to improve your relationships. This year I noted that I wanted to go on three individual dates with one of my sons. Of course these dates are in addition to making an all-round effort to draw closer to him, but I recognised the need for some focussed time outside the house. Sometimes one person needs a bit more than others, and that's okay. Note that, if you fail to plan an adjustment, the year is much more likely to end much the same as the previous one, or worse. Maybe you need to increase the amount of time you spend with your grandparents or invite siblings around for dinner.

The more time you take to do a yearly review and unpack your goals for the coming year, the more useful it will be. Do this together with a spouse or friend and make it fun. It's not meant to be a negative experience, but more on a motivating one.

Ways to Save on Home Improvements

~

Every now and again it is a nice idea to revamp the home even if just a little bit. Remember we want our home to be a place that is not only warm and inviting but one where we feel motivated and re-energised. You would be amazed at what a fresh lick of paint or new pair of curtains can do for a space. For some of us this may seem like a potentially costly endeavour but there are a few ways in which we can avoid splashing the cash. From the outset let me just say that there are some things that simply need a professional! Under no circumstances should you attempt anything that could put your health or home at risk so for the sake of yourself and everyone else, leave the electrics alone! Admit defeat when the job is beyond you or a member of your household and save up to get the job done properly. However, with a bit of time and creativity there are some things that anyone can achieve.

Change up accessories for a fresh look

Instead of making expensive changes to your home, consider whether simply replacing a few furnishing items or introducing a new colour could achieve the itch that needs scratching. It is usually inexpensive to replace items such as picture frames, cushion covers, vases or candles. You could even colour co-ordinate with things like pot pouri, home fresheners or seasonal flowers. Go for natural tones in the autumn, deeper, richer ones for winter, pastels for spring and brighter vibrant colours for summer.

Frame interesting pictures, artwork or photos

Following on from the last point, you could consider framing something other than a family photo to give your home an eclectic feel. You can literally frame anything! Why not write out your favourite poem or quote in your best handwriting or print it in a pretty font from the computer? How about framing your children's artwork or Mother's Day card they made you? Magazine clippings of holiday destinations or city skylines, a map of the world, antique photos, a page from a religious book of even the family name can make great wall art.

Get creative with a project

If you're good with your hands you may want to consider an easy DIY project. There are so many suggestions and tutorials on YouTube or Pinterest you could have fun attempting. A friend of mine recently made a canopy to hang above her daughter's bed using the simplest of equipment. It took less than half an hour and cost next to nothing. The possibilities are endless when it comes to creative projects and options range from easy stuff like hand prints, to the more complicated things like tie dying for example. There are even stores which specialise in providing how-to kits with step by step instructions for you to follow.

Have a DIY or Gardening "Party"

Sometimes a job is far too big for you to do all by yourself so you need hands to help. Instead of paying a handy man to clear the weeds and cut down overgrown plants in the garden you could opt for ten of your friends. Invite them round with the understanding that they are there to help you achieve something. So in this case it would be to clear the garden. Make sure there is food and drinks provided for them and let everyone get stuck in. Many hands make light work as they say.

Up cycling and Repair

Could you reinforce your breakfast bar stools yourself? Sometimes we are hasty to replace items of furniture when all they need is a few replacement screws or a fresh coat of varnish. Think long and hard before rushing out to buy a new chest of draws because all the handles have fallen off. A new set would probably only cost you a few pounds and are quick to install once you know how. You could also use broken or unwanted furniture as parts for building something else. Admittedly this requires a bit more expertise so don't attempt if it's a bit ambitious. When my husband was making new built in wardrobes for the children's bedrooms, he used the wood from their old broken wardrobes to build some cubby shelves inside. Very little ended up being wasted.

The point I want to reiterate here is to put the family's collective skills to use. If someone can sew a bit, cushions and covers are very easy with a how-to guide from the internet. Together, you can save a fair bit of money by doing things yourself. Remember to get a professional in for anything that you require specialist help with. Even the disposal of simple things like builder's rubble or old paint must be done safely and sometimes by a licenced disposal company.

Final thoughts

~

It is my hope that this book has been of some use to you. My heart has been to share what I have tried and tested and to give you some insight on how you can go about managing the huge blessing that is your home. Be diligent to implement anything that you have gained to help improve the quality of your home. It is our responsibility as manager to teach and train the next generation. Even if you have no biological children, you can share with other women (and men) so they are equipped with lifelong skills too. Don't be fooled into thinking that knowing how to care for a home is something that is demeaning or silly. After all, we all want to dwell somewhere that makes our world better. This will only happen if you are deliberate in learning year on year. I still have much to learn and this has only been highlighted further whilst writing this book. The seemingly never-ending list of things to do is worth it because let's face it, a clean and organised home is just nicer to exist in.

Keeping up with the housework and general upkeep makes guests feel more welcome and reduces the stress of not being able to find anything. So keep going, your hard work is not in vain. I am convinced that it is making a difference in your life and in the lives of your family.

With much blessings

Nichola -x-

Bibliography

Visual, Auditory, Kinaesthetic Learning Styles and
Their Impacts on English Language Teaching
Abbas Pourhossein Gilakjani, 2012

Carrier Bags - Why there's a charge
Department for Environment, Food and Rural Affairs -
Gov.uk - Dec 2015

Wedded your way officiant services
weddedyourway.com

10 things you may not know about laughter – Dr Mercola
– November 13, 2014

10 Benefits of Managing your Money
Budgetingincome.com – 2013

10 Benefits of a Good Night's Sleep – Mark Stibich –
Verywell.com - May 4, 2016

See If Your Kid Is Going to Sleep at the Right Time Based on This Viral Bedtime Chart – Kate Schweitzer – popsuger.com - June 25, 2016

Family Spending

3. Household Expenditure in 2014

www.ons.gov.uk

Money Languages - Marriage Today, Jimmy Evans – YouTube.com – June 26 2012

Money Language: What is it? – Lorrie Millet - popcheetahlife.com – March 14, 2013

Other titles from Nichola Williams

The Altar: A true story of faith, love, life and death [2015]
Paperback and Kindle formats available on Amazon
websites worldwide